MAKING OUT IN CHINESE

MAKING OUT IN CHINESE

BY RAY DANIELS

YENBOOKS

To Shiau Ray—Good luck in your studies, son!
Thank you Ling Yuen, Sho Jean, and Sho Ling.

Illustrated by Jude Brand

YENBOOKS
2-6 Suido 1-chome, Bunkyo-ku, Tokyo 112

LCC Card No. 93-60059
ISBN 0-8048-1863-0

First edition, 1993
Second printing, 1994

Printed in Japan

CONTENTS

INTRODUCTION

The idea behind *Making Out in Chinese* is to aid those who wish to speak real Chinese rather than the dry textbook style taught all over the world. No one really speaks textbook English, and the same is true of Chinese, so why not make out using real everyday Chinese? I hope this work saves students valuable study time so that they can quickly move on to communicate naturally. My dream is that all of you who are enlightened by the words within will be successful in your attempts at making out in Chinese.

INFORMATION

Customs, habits, and traditions vary greatly throughout the world, and the traveler must take this into consideration when encountering other cultures. In my travels throughout China, I often heard the expression: *Nǐ-mèn shî-fāng rén hǔn kāi-fàng. Wǒ-mèn jōng-gúo rén hǔn bów-shǒ* (You Westerners are very liberal. We Chinese are very conservative). The forwardness of Western men and women, particularly in dealings with the opposite sex, has left many Chinese with the impression that Westerners are lacking in morals. If you are amorously interested in a Chinese, or just want to make friends, an indirect approach is recommended. It's better to give subtle hints about your feelings rather than just come out with them directly. The more subtle you are, the more well-intentioned you will seem.

The phrases in this book will be comprehensible in all Chinese-speaking countries. However, the degree of openness, especially in sexual matters, differs from country to country. My own personal ranking, from most liberal to most conservative, is as follows: Hong Kong, mainland China, Macao, Taiwan, Singapore, Malaysia. My high ranking of mainland China may surprise some, but a great deal of openness is due to the number of Chinese seeking a foreign partner (and passport!).

PRONUNCIATION TIPS

All words in Chinese have a tone, and an incorrect tonal pronunciation can greatly change the word's meaning. For example:

First tone: The word *mā* spoken with first tone means mother. The first tone is an even pitched sound, almost like singing.

Second tone: The word *má* with second tone means hemp. The second tone rises, like one would say the word "right?"

Third tone: The word *mǎ* spoken with the third tone means horse. It is pronounced with a lowering of the voice.

Fourth tone: The word mà with fourth tone means to scold someone. For instance, if one were to swear at someone, one would *"Mà!"* said individual. The fourth tone is spoken sharply, like the word "Damn!"

There is one more tone, *mà,* referred to by the Chinese as "light sound," which indicates that the syllable should be spoken like the fourth tone pronunciation of the word "Damn!" except shorter (as if the speaker had tried to say "Damn!" but only had time to pronounce the "da").

I advise the reader not to worry about the tones but to concentrate on the pronunciations which have been written so that English speakers can pronounce them easily. Just as English is spoken with different accents, so is Chinese; learners of Chinese must therefore develop an ear for the language.

VOWELS

a	Like the "a" in father.
e	Like the "e" in hen.
i	Like the "i" in pin. A single letter "i" is pronounced like the "e" in he.
o	Like the "o" in snow.
u	Like the "u" in July.
ai	Pronounced like eye.
an	Pronounced like the "an" in Khan.
au	Pronounced like the "ow" of how.
ay	Pronounced like the "ay" in hay.

er Pronounced like the "ear" of Early.
ow Pronounced like the "ow" of how.
uh Pronounced like the "u" of ugly.
un Pronounced like the "un" of nun.

Consonants and other sounds are pronounced as in English.

TENSES

Tenses are expressed simply in Chinese. If you want to express that you already did something, you can add the word *lùh* at the end of the sentence. If you wish to express that you will do something, you can use the words *jiāng huày*. For example: I will go, is *Wǒ jiāng huày chìu*. A sentence can also be made past or future by the use of time words such as *míng tiēn* (tomorrow) or *dzúo tiēn* (yesterday). Time is usually mentioned at the beginning of a sentence. For example, I will go tomorrow: *Wǒ míng tiēn chìu*. I went yesterday: *Wǒ dzúo tiēn chìu lùh*.

BASIC PHRASES

Who?	*Sháy?*
What?	*Shém-mùh?*
Where?	*Nár-lǐ?*
When?	*Shém-mùh shér-hò?*
Why?	*Wày shém-mùh?*
How?	*Rú-héh?*
Whose?	*Sháy dùh?*
This.	*Jùh-gùh.*
That.	*Nàh-gùh.*
Here.	*Jùh-lǐ.*
There.	*Nàh-lǐ.*
If.	*Rú-guǒ.*

But.	*Dàn-shèr.* *Kŭh-shèr.* *Bú-guò.*
Because.	*Īng-wày.*
Thus.	*Nàh-mùh.*
So. Therefore.	*Suó-ĭ.*
Yes.	*Shèr dùh.* *Shèr.*
No.	*Bú shèr dùh.* *Bù.*
Maybe, might.	*Yeáh-shĭu.* *Kŭh-núng.*
Maybe not, might not.	*Kŭh-núng bú shèr.*
I.	*Wŏ.*
You.	*Nĭ.*
He/she/it.	*Tā.*
We.	*Wŏ-mèn.*
You (plural).	*Nĭ-mèn.*

They.	*Tā-mèn.*
The verb "to be."	*Shèr.*
I ____ it.	*Wǒ ____ dòw lùh.*
Don't ____.	*Bú yòw ____.*
Did you ____ it?	*Nǐ ____ dòw lùh mà?*
I didn't ____ it.	*Wǒ máy ____ dòw.*
I couldn't ____ it.	*Wǒ bù núng ____ dòw.*
I want to ____ it.	*Wó shiǎng ____.*
I don't want to ____ it.	*Wǒ bù shiǎng ____.*

Hear, listen.	*Tīng.*
See, look.	*Kàn.*
Smell.	*Wén.*
Touch.	*Pòng.* *Mūo.*
Listen to me!	*Tīng wǒ shuō!*
Have you seen Lee?	*Nǐ kàn dòw Lée mà?*
I saw Lee.	*Wǒ kàn dòw Lée lùh.*
I want to see you!	*Wó shiǎng chìu kàn nǐ!*
I'll show it to you.	*Wǒ gáy nǐ kàn.*
Please (polite).	*Chǐng.*
Please (begging).	*Bài-tuō.**

* Also means "please" as in "What do you take me for?"

Thank you.	*Shièh-shièh.*
You're welcome.	*Bú kùh-chi.* *Beáh kùh-chi.* *Bú-shièh.*

Where is the bathroom?	*Tsùh-suǒ zài nǎr?* *Huàh juāng shèr zài nǎr?**

* This is to locate the "powder room" and is for women only.

What is this?	*Jùh shèr shém-mùh?*
What is this/that called?	*Jùh-gùh/Nàh-gùh jiòw shém-mùh?*
What does ____ mean?	*____ shèr shém-mùh ì-sż?*
How do you pronounce this?	*Jùh gùh dzěm-mùh nièn?*
I have a question.	*Wó yǒ í-gùh wèn-tí.*
Do you understand?	*Dǒng bù dǒng?* *Ní dǒng mà?*
I don't understand.	*Wó bù dǒng.*
I understand.	*Wó dǒng.*
Please explain.	*Chíng jǐeh shèr.* *Chǐng shūo míng.*
Complex.	*Fù-záh.*

Simple, easy.	*Jiěn-dāng.*
Difficult.	*Kwèn-nàn.*
No wonder.	*Guài bù dúh.*
It's obvious.	*Kéh shiǎng ér jîr.*
I know.	*Wǒ jēr-dòw.*
I don't know.	*Wǒ bù jēr-dòw.*
I forgot.	*Wǒ wàng-jì lùh.*
I remember.	*Wǒ jì-dùh.*

Tell me.	*Gòw-sù wǒ.*
What did you say?	*Nǐ shuō shém-mùh?*
Is it OK ?	*Hǒw bù hǒw?* *Kéh-ǐ mà?*
Is it OK to do it?	*Shíng bù shíng?* *Shíng mà?*
No way (you don't have permission).	*Bù shíng!*
Have permission.	*Shíng.*
Either is OK .	*Dōh kúh-ǐ.*
Is this right?	*Dwày bù dwày?*
Right.	*Dwày.*
By the way.	*Dwày lùh.* *Shùen-bien shuō.*
Wrong.	*Bú dwày.*
Success.	*Chún gōng.*
Failure.	*Shēr bài.*
Almost.	*Jī-hù*

Same.	*Ì-yàng.*
About the same.	*Chā bù-duō.*
Imitate.	*Múo fáng.*
I have trouble! I'm in trouble!	*Wó yǒ má-fán!*
What's wrong with you?	*Ní dzěm-mùh lùh?*
What's wrong?	*Yǒ shém-mùh wèn-tí?*
Nothing's wrong!	*Máy wèn-tí bà!*
You aren't hurt, are you? Are you OK?	*Nǐ máy shèr bà?*
Do you need help?	*Nǐ shîu yòw bāng-jù mà?*
I need help.	*Wǒ shîu yòw bāng-jù.*
I don't need help.	*Wǒ bù shîu yòw bāng-jù.*
I'll help you do it.	*Wǒ bāng nǐ dzùo.*
Help me.	*Bāng wǒ í shìah.*
Help!	*Jiòu-mìng!*

Be careful! Look out!	*Shiǎu shîn!*
Dangerous.	*Wáy-shǐen.*
Careless.	*Bù shiǎu shîn.*
I'm sick.	*Wǒ bù shū fù.*
Where is the hospital?	*Ī-yuèn zài nǎr?*
How much?	*Duō shǎu?*
Buy it!	*Mǎi shiàh lái!*
I don't want to buy it.	*Wǒ bú yòw mǎi.*
It's too expensive!	*Tài guày lùh.*

Very poor quality.	*Hŭn làn.*
Give me a cheaper price.	*Swàn pién-í diěn.*
Do you want it?	*Yòw bù yòw?*
I want ____.	*Wŏ yòw ____.*
I don't want ____.	*Wŏ bú yòw ____.*
Please give me change.	*Chǐng gáy wŏ huàn líng-chíen.*
Enough?	*Gò lùh mà?*
Enough.	*Gò lùh.*
Not enough.	*Bú gò.*
Satisfied?	*Mán-ì mà?*
Satisfied.	*Mán-ì.*
Not satisfied.	*Bù mán-ì.*
Separate.	*Fēn-kāi.*
Put together.	*Fàng zài ì-chǐ.*
All together.	*Í-gòng.*

It's OK (acceptable).	*Hái kéh-ĭ.*
Give it to me.	*Gáy wŏ.*
Here, take it.	*Náh chìu bà.*
Hold this.	*Náh jùh.*
I have ____.	*Wó yŏ ____.*
I don't have ____.	*Wŏ máy yŏ ____.*
What is next?	*Jîeh shiàh lái nùh?*
Last time.	*Shàng tsž.*
This time.	*Jày tsž.*
Next time.	*Shiàh tsž.*
A long time ago.	*Hún jioŭ í-chíen.*
Just a moment ago.	*Gāng tsái.*
After.	*Ĭ-hò.*
Before.	*Ĭ-chíen.*
Time.	*Shér-hò.* *Shér-jiēn.*

What time? (When?)	*Shém-mùh shér-hò?*
What time is it (now)?	*Shìen zài jí-diĕn?*
Sometimes.	*Yŏ shér hò.*
Always.	*Zŏng-shèr.* *Jîng-cháng.*
Seldom.	*Ó-ér.*
Never.	*Tsóng lái máy yŏ.*
Not even once.	*Í-tsz dōh máy yŏ.*
Forever.	*Yŏng yuén.*
Please fix ____.	*Chĭng shioū-lĭ ____.*
Of course.	*Dāng rán.*
Convenient.	*Fāng-bìen.*
Not convienent.	*Bù fāng-bìen.*
Definitely. For sure.	*Í-dìng.*
Not definitely/not necessarily.	*Bù í-dìng.*

It's impossible.	*Bù kŭh-núng.*
It's possible.	*Kŭh-núng.*
No patience.	*Máy nài shîn.*
No confidence.	*Máy shìn shîn.*
Don't worry!	*Bú yòw dān-shîn!*
Be happy!	*Kwài-lùh ì-diĕn!*
Happy.	*Tòng kwài.*
Lucky.	*Yuìn -chèe hŏw.*
Unlucky.	*Dŏw-máy.*

Getting Acquainted 2

What's your family name?   *Nín guày shìng?**

> *This is a very polite way to ask someone's name and should be said when meeting someone for the first time. *Nín* is an especially polite form of "you," and *gùay* means honorable.

What's your name?

Nǐ jiòw shém-mùh míng-dż?

Hi, how's it going?
What's up ?
How are you?

Ní hǒw mà?

How's it going?
How is it?

Dzěm-mùh yàng?

How have you been lately?

Nǐ dzùay jìn dzěm-mùh yàng?

I'm fine.

Wǒ hún hǒw.

I'm happy.

Wó hǔn kwài-lùh.

I feel sad.	*Wŏ juáy-dùh nán-guò.*
I feel tired.	*Wŏ juáy-dùh lày.*
I've got a headache.	*Wŏ tó tòng.*
I feel sick.	*Wŏ juáy dùh bù shū-fù.*
I'm sleepy.	*Wó shiăng shùay-jiòw.*
What have you been up to lately?	*Dzùay jìn máng shém-mùh?*
Long time no see.	*Hów jĭo bú-jièn.**

* This statement was originally Chinese and has become an English expression. It is a literal translation.

My Chinese/English is poor.	*Wŏ-dùh Jōng-wén/ Īng-wén bù hŏw.*
Please speak in English.	*Chíng jiăng Īng-wén.*
Please speak in Chinese.	*Chíng jiăng Jōng-wén.*
Please speak slower.	*Chĭng shuō màn ì-diĕn.*
Please say it again.	*Chĭng zài shuō í-bièn.*
What do you mean?	*Nĭ shèr shém-mùh ì-sż?*

What do you want to say?	*Nǐ yòw shuō shém-mùh?*
Please come in.	*Chǐng jìn.*
Do you want to sit down?	*Nǐ yòw dzuò mà?*
Please sit down.	*Chǐng dzuò.*
May I sit down?	*Wǒ kúh-ǐ dzuò mà?*
Someone is sitting here.	*Jùh gùh wày-dž yǒ rén dzuò.*
Where are you from?	*Nǐ tsóng nǎr lái dùh?*
What do you do for a living?	*Nǐ dzuò shém-mùh gōng-dzùo?*
How old are you?	*Ní jǐ swày?* Nín duō dàh?***

* For children.
** For adults.

How long have you been here?	*Nǐ dzài jèr dūo jǐou lùh?*
What are you interested in?	*Ní yǒ shém-mùh shìng-chìu?*

What is your hobby?	*Nǐ-dùh shìng-chìu shèr shém-mùh?*
I'm interested in ____.	*Wó-dùh shìng-chìu shèr ____.* *Wǒ dwày ____ yǒ shìng-chìu.*
I'm interested in it.	*Wó dwày jùh gùh yǒ shìng-chìu.*
I'm not interested in it.	*Wǒ máy shìng-chìu.*
It means nothing to me.	*Bú swàn shém-mùh.*
I like ____.	*Wó shǐ-huān ____.*
I like it.	*Wó shǐ-huān.*
I don't like ____.	*Wǒ bù shǐ-huān ____.*

I don't like it.

Wǒ bù shǐ-huān.

I hate ____.

Wó tǎu-yièn ____.

I loathe ____.

*Wǒ hùn ____.**

  * Very strong statement and is seldom said.

Have you done ____
    before?

*Ní ǐ-chíen dzuò ____
guò mà?
Ní ǐ-chíen dzuò guò
____mà?*

What religion are you?

*Nǐ shìn shém-mùh
jiòw?*

Buddhism.

Fó jiòw.

Christianity.

Jî-dū jiòw.

Islam.

*Ī-sū-lán jiòw.
Huáy jiòw.*

Taoism.

Dòw jiòw.

Catholicism.

Tiēn jǔ jiòw.

Atheist.

Wú shén luèn jǔh.

No religion.

Bú shìn jiòw.

Sleep.   *Shùay jiòw.**

   * This is a common joke as sleep sounds like a
   religion. Notice the ending *jiòw*.

What's your blood type?   *Nǐ shèr shém-mùh*
                             shǐeh shíng?*

   * In Asia, this is an important indicator of your
   personality.

Type A: Tender, neat, and kind. They make
          good wives.

Type B: Loving, cute, active, and humorous.

Type O: Bad tempered, good decision makers.
          They are typical leaders and are wise.
          They make good elder brothers.

Type AB: Weird geniuses. Sometimes thought to
          be crazy and emotional.

I'm (A) type.   *Wǒ shèr (Ā) shín.*

What's your year sign?   **Ní shǔ shém-mùh?*

   *This is concerned with Chinese astrology. Each year
   is denoted by one of twelve different animals. Your
   year-animal is an indicator of your personality.

My year sign is____.   *Wó shǔ* ____.

Mouse.   *Shǔ.*

Ox.   *Nioú.*

Tiger.   *Hǔ.*

Rabbit.   *Tù.*

Dragon.   *Lóng.*

Snake.   *Súh.*

Horse.   *Mǎ.*

Sheep.   *Yáng.*

Monkey.   *Hó.*

Cock (chicken).   *Jî.*

Dog.   *Gǒ.*

Pig.   *Jū.*

How the Chinese Astrology System Was Created

Long, long ago, there was no concept of time. There were no clocks or calendars. People wanted to mark the passing of time but didn't know how. So, they sought advice from the Emperor, known for his wisdom in such matters. He pondered for considerable time before deigning to offer his learned advice: "Because animals and humans have a close affinity and the names of animals are easily remembered, they should be used to symbolize time. Henceforth, a river-crossing race shall be held to determine those animals best suited to signify time."

Thereupon the event was held. All manner of beast attended. The cat and the mouse, who were good friends, discussed the best manner in which to cross, as neither could swim. They decided to ask the ox to aid them. The ox, being a sincere and kindhearted soul, agreed to carry them across. The race began and the ox, who was by far the best swimmer, emerged in the lead. As they neared the finish line, the cat proudly rose and declared the three of them to be the first to cross the line. But the mouse, a cunning and selfish soul, secretly desired to cross the line first. So he caught the cat unawares and pushed him into the water. He then jumped behind the ox's ear. The ox, unaware of the commotion, swam on to the finish line. Just as he reached the shore, the mouse leaped forward and ran to victory, quickly followed by the ox, the tiger, the rabbit [1], the dragon [2], the snake [3], the horse [3], the sheep [4], the monkey [4], the cock [4], the dog [4], and the pig [5]. The exhausted cat finally scrambled to shore, but the race was already over. The cat was extremely angry at the mouse, and every time they met, the cat tried to bite him. He then reported the mouse's crime to all of his progeny, beginning a feud between the two animals which continues to this very day. The mouse, knowing full-well of his sin, skulked away in guilt and spent the rest of his days hiding in dark, sullen places.

[1] The rabbit, who could not swim, made the crossing by leaping across the other animals' heads. He acquired his peculiarly-shaped mouth because he ran too fast, and after crossing the finish line, ran into a tree.

[2] The dragon, who should have placed higher in the race, had been busy in the heavens creating thunder and lighting. He absent-mindedly made the thunder too loud, which caused him to become fairly deaf. As a consequence, he did not hear the start of the race and had to come from behind to acquire fifth place.

[3] The snake, in order to defeat the horse, scared him and dashed in front. Unfortunately for him, he ran too fast, causing his four legs to break off, and leaving him in his present legless state.

[4] The sheep, monkey, and cock had agreed to make the crossing together. They did so by

putting the sheep on the shoulders of the monkey, who in turn sat upon the back of the cock. As they were crossing, the sheep (who was a sort of lookout), saw the dog (who was naughtily bathing in the river) and scolded him severely. The dog continued the race and finished next to last but he didn't really care. The sheep ended up over-straining his eyes and permanently damaged his vision. The monkey, who sat far too long, acquired a permanently red posterior. The cock, who had been supporting the group, lost two of his original four legs as they were crushed.

[5] The pig finished dead last as he decided to finish eating before crossing the river. When he finally made it across, he began entreating the emperor for more food. His gluttony caused him to become the laughing stock of all those present.

Year* and Personalities

*The animal years repeat every twelve years.

1993. Cock: Proud, enthusiastic, stylish, popular, lively, amusing, generous, adventurous, industrious, conservative, courageous.
Pompous, pedantic, short-sighted, boastful, mistrustful, extravagant.

1994. Dog: Faithful, loyal, noble, modest, devoted, prosperous, courageous, respectable, selfless, dutiful, intelligent.
Introverted, cynical, critical, moralizing, stubborn, defensive.

1995. Pig: Scrupulous, loyal, sincere, honest, loving, sociable, sensitive, sensual, truthful, peaceful, intelligent.
Naive, Epicurean, insecure, gullible, defenseless, non-competitive, earthy.

1996. Mouse: Aggressive, energetic, jolly, charming, sociable, humorous, generous, intellectual, sentimental, honest, persistent.
Greedy, small-minded, power-hungry, destructive, suspicious, tiresome, likes to gamble.

1997. Ox: Hard-working, lonely, leaders, strong, proud, reserved, methodical, original, eloquent, patient, silent.

Rigid, bad losers, authoritarian, conventional, jealous, stubborn, slow.

1998. Tiger: Smiling, magnetic, lucky, strong, honorable, good leaders, liberal-minded, courageous, generous, passionate.
Vain, rash, disobedient, undisciplined, argumentative, rebellious.

1999. Rabbit: Cautious, clever, hospitable, sociable, friendly, sensitive, ambitious, careful, private.
Timid, thin-skinned, old-fashioned, hypochondriac, squeamish.

2000. Dragon: Showy, artistic, enthusiastic, lucky, healthy, generous, sentimental, successful, independent.
Demanding, irritable, loud-mouthed, stubborn, discontented, willful. The dragon is the symbol of the emperor.

2001. Snake: Wise, sympathetic, lucky, sophisticated, calm, decisive, attractive, philosophical, elegant, compassionate.
Lazy, possessive, tight-fisted, bad losers, changeable, vengeful, extravagant.

2002. Horse: Gifted, athletic, charming, quick-witted, hard-working, entertaining, powerful, skillful, cheerful, eloquent, independent.

Weak, unfeeling, hot-headed, selfish, ruthless, tactless, impatient, rebellious.

2003. Sheep: Gentle, artistic, peace-loving, sweet-natured, lovable, creative, inventive, amorous, tasteful, intelligent.
Insecure, pessimistic, unpunctual, undisicpined, dissatisfied, irresponsible.

2004. Monkey: Merry, enthusiastic, witty, good in business, clever, fascinating, passionate, youthful, very intelligent, inventive.
Vain, adolescent, long-winded, unfaithful, untruthful, untrustworthy.

What's your Astrological sign?	*Nǐ shèr shém-mùh shîng dzuò?*
Aries.	*Bái-yáng dzuò.*
Taurus.	*Jîn-nióu dzuò.*
Gemini.	*Shuāng-dž dzuò.*
Cancer.	*Jiù-shièh dzuò.*
Leo.	*Shēr-dż dzuò.*
Virgo.	*Chú-niǔ dzuò.*

Libra.	*Tiēn-píng dzuò.*
Scorpio.	*Tiēn-shièh dzuò.*
Sagittarius.	*Shùh-shǐo dzuò.* *Rén-mǎ dzuò.*
Capricorn.	*Múo-shiēh dzuò.*
Aquarius.	*Shǔay-píng dzuò.* *Bǎu-píng dzùo.*
Pisces.	*Yíu dzuò.* *Shuāng-yíu dzuò.*
Do you believe it?	*Nǐ shiāng shìn mà?*
It might be true.	*Kǔh núng shèr jēn-dùh.*

I believe it!	*Wǒ shiāng-shìn!*
I don't believe it!	*Wǒ bù shiāng-shìn!*
Really?	*Jēn-dùh mà?*
That's a lie!	*Nàh shèr hwǎng-hwàh!*
You lied!	*Nǐ shuō hwǎng!*
Tell the truth!	*Shuō jēn-dùh!*
How do you know?	*Ní dzěm-mùh jēr dòw?*
Who said it?	*Sháy shuō dùh?*
I know that person.	*Wǒ rèn-shèr nàh gùh rén.*
I know him/her.	*Wǒ rèn-shèr tā.*
It depends.	*Kàn chíng-shíng.*
I agree with you.	*Wǒ tóng-ì.*
I don't agree with you.	*Wǒ bù tóng-ì.*
I didn't think of that.	*Wǒ máy shiǎng dòw.*

I didn't consider that.	*Wǒ máy kǎu-lìu guò.*
I figured that.	*Wǒ jiòu jēr dòw.*
Our thinking is the same.	*Wǒ-mèn dùh shiáng-fǎh shiāng-tóng.*
Do you care?	*Nǐ zài-hū mà?*
Do you care about ____?	*Nǐ zài-hū ____ mà?*
I don't care.	*Wǒ bú zài-hū.*
Who cares?	*Sháy zài-hū?*
Either is fine.	*Dōh kúh-ǐ.*
No problem.	*Máy wèn-tí.*
It doesn't matter.	*Máy guān-shi.*
Go for it!	*Chìu dzuò bà!*
I've got a way (to do/solve something)	*Wó yǒ bàn-fǎh.*
What way?	*Shém-mùh bàn-fǎh?*
There's no way you can do it!	*Nǐ máy bàn-fǎh!*

It can't be helped. There's nothing we can do about it.	*Máy bàn-fǎh.*
Why did you do that?	*Nǐ wày shém-mùh dzèm-mùh dzuò?*
Let's start it.	*Kāi-shěr bà.*
Finished.	*Dzuò hǒw lùh.*
Finished?	*Dzuò hǒw lùh mā?*
Do you have free time?	*Yǒ kòng mà?*
Would you like to go (to) ____?	*Ní shiǎng chìu ____?*
Bar (pub).	*Jiǒu-bā.*
Park.	*Gōng-yuén.*
Jogging.	*Màn pǒw.*
Swimming.	*Yó-yǒng.*
Restaurant.	*Tsān-tîng.*
Let's go see a movie!	*Wǒ-mèn chìu kàn dièn-ǐng!*

Have you seen ____ before?

Nǐ kàn guò ____ mā?

Movie.

Dièn-ǐng.

What kind of movie would you like to watch?

Ní shǐ-huān kàn shém-mùh dièn-ǐng?

Two tickets please.

Chǐng gáy wó liǎng jāng piòw.

Science Fiction.

Kūh-huàn pièn.

Comedy.

Shǐ-jiù pièn.

Romance.

Aì-chíng wén-ì pièn.
Wén-ì pièn.

Horror.	*Kǒng-bù pièn.*
Ghost.	*Guǎy-guài pièn.*
Adventure.	*Dòng-dzuò pièn.*
Gangster.	*Jíng-feǐ pièn.*
Mystery.	*Shún-guài pièn.*
Western.	*Shî-bù pièn.*
X-rated.	*Hwáng-sùh dièn-ǐng.** *Sùh chíng pièn.*

* *Hwáng sùh* means yellow, the Chinese version of the Western red-light district.

American/European movie.	*Shî-yáng pièn.*
Chinese movie.	*Jōng-wén pièn.*
Good idea.	*Hów jǔ-i.*
Let me think it over.	*Ràng wó shiǎng í-shiàh.*
Have you decided yet?	*Nǐ juáy-dìng lùh mà?*
It's up to you.	*Swáy-bièn nǐ.*

You decide.	*Nǐ juáy-dìng.*
When can you ____?	*Nǐ shém-mùh shér-hò kúh-ǐ ____?*
Come.	*Lái.*
Go.	*Chìu.*
Do it.	*Dzuò.*
Do you want to go?	*Ní shiǎng chìu mà?*
I can't go.	*Wǒ bù núng chìu.*
Are you ready?	*Hǒw lùh máy yǒ?*
Ready.	*Hǒw lùh.*
Not ready. Not yet.	*Hái máy.*
Meet me at ____.	*Wǒ-mèn zài ____ jièn.*
I'll wait for you.	*Wǒ dúng nǐ.*
I won't leave until you come.	*Bú jièn bú sàn.*
Please don't stand me up!	*Chǐng bú yòw fàng wǒ gūh-dż!*

Let's go!	*Wǒ-mèn zǒ bà!*
Do you have a phone?	*Ní yǒ dièn-hwàh mà?*
What's your phone number?	*Nǐ dùh dièn-hwàh jǐ hòw?*
Can I call you?	*Wǒ kéh-í dǎh dièn hwàh gáy nǐ mà?*

On the phone:

Hello, is ____ there?	*Wáy, chǐng-wèn ____ zài mà?*
Please give me extension ____.	*Chíng juǒn ____.*
The telephone line is busy.	*Jàn-shìen.*
Who's calling please?	*Chǐng-wèn, nǐ shèr nǎh wày?*
Please hold on for a moment.	*Chíng dǔng í-shiàh.*
____ isn't in.	*____ bú zài.*
When will he/she be back?	*Tā shém-mùh shér-hò hwáy lái?*

Please tell him/her ____ called.	*Chǐng gòw-sù tā ____ dǎ dièn-hwà gǎy tā.*
Please tell him/her ____.	*Chǐng gòw-sù tā ____.*
I will phone again.	*Wǒ zài dǎ dièn-hwà lái.*
I'll call you.	*Wó dǎh dièn hwà gáy nǐ.*
Please call me.	*Chíng dǎh dièn hwà gáy wǒ.*
Please have him/her call me.	*Chǐng jiòw tā hwáy dièn gáy wǒ.*
My phone number is ____.	*Wǒ-dùh dièn-hwà hòw-mǎ shèr ____.*

I'll call you back.	*Wǒ hwáy dièn gáy nǐ.*
Please give me a ride (to ____).	*Chíng nǐ zài wǒ (dòw ____ chìu).*
Can you come here?	*Nǐ kéh-ǐ lái jùh-lǐ mà?*
Where do you live?	*Nǐ jù nǎr?*
What's your address?	*Nǐ dùh dì-jěr zài nǎr?*
Please write it down.	*Chíng shǐeh shiàh lái.*
I'll see you home.	*Wǒ sòng nǐ hwáy jiāh.*
Watch your step.	*Màn zǒ.**

*Literally means "walk slowly" and is commonly used. The response is *Hǒw.*

I'll write you a letter.	*Wǒ hwày shǐeh shìn gáy nǐ.*
If you have free time, let's get together.	*Yǒ kòng, jièn.*
I'll leave first.	*Wǒ shiēn zǒ.*
See you in a while.	*Hwáy tó jièn.*
See you later.	*Gaǐ tiēn jièn.*

See you tomorrow.   *Míng-tiēn jièn.*

See you tonight.   *Wǎn-shàng jièn.*

Come back sometime!   *Zài lái!*

Good bye.   *Zài-jièn.*

Shooting
the Breeze

Bullshit!	*Fày-hwàh!* *Fàng-pì!** *Luàn-jiǎng!***

* literally means "Fart!"
** Women's expression.

Flatterer (person who talks a lot of bull).	*Chūay nióu.*

Flattery.	*Pāi mǎ pì.**

* literally means to pat the horse's rear end.

Smart alek.	*Dǎ pì.*

Common Chinese.	*Pǔ-tōng hwàh.**

* This refers to ordinary, everyday spoken Chinese.

Weird, bizarre, strange.	*Chée-guài.*

I'm sick of ____.	*Woáh hǔn fán ____.*

Boring.	*Wú-lióu.*
Be cheated (ripped off).	*Shàng dàng.* *Bày pièn.*
To be at a disadvantage or to suffer a loss.	*Chēr kuāy.*
Don't let others cheat you!	*Beáh shàng dàng!*
That really makes me laugh!	*Jēn hǒw shiàu!*
Is it fun?	*Hǒw wán mà?*
Is it funny?	*Hǒw shiàu mà?*
What are you laughing at?	*Shiàu shém-mùh?*
That's really interesting!	*Yǒ ì-sż!*
Continue.	*Jì-shìu.*
And then?	*Rán hò nàh?*
Bizarre guy (person who does things differently from everyone else—so much so that he draws a lot of unwanted attention).	*Aì dzuò guài.*

Frighteningly ugly person!   *Kǔh bù!**

> * This is a contraction of two Chinese words *Kǔh pà* meaning frightening and *Kǔng bù* meaning horrible.

Who farted?	*Sháy fùng-pì lüh?*
Guess!	*Tsāi tsāi kàn!*
You did!	*Jìou shèr nǐ!*
Embarrassed.	*Bù hǒw ì-sż.*
Damn it (I screwed up)!	*Zōw lùh!*
I can't stand ____!	*Wǒ shoù bù-liǒw ____!*
Mysterious-acting person.	*Shén mì shî shî.*
Person with a jovial face.	*Shiàu shī shī.*
Pitiful-looking face.	*Kǔ-guāh liěn.*
Mean face.	*Bǎn-jùh liěn.*
Leader. (Male).	*Dà-gūh dà.**
(Female).	*Dà-jiěh tó.***

> * Literally big brother. It's also used for Mafia bosses and cordless telephones.
>
> ** Literally big sister.

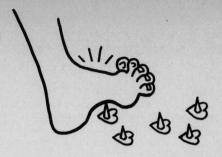

| How pitiful! | *Hów kŭh-lién!** |
| | *Hów kŭh-shî!*** |

* Used for people

** Used for things.

| Tender foot. | *Tsài niŏw.** |

* This is for a beginner at something.

| Experienced person. | *Láu niŏw.* |

| Person who loves to show off. | *Aì chū fōng tó.* |

| Good, kind, man. | *Hów hŏw shiuāh shūng.* |

| Person who has many talents. | *Liáng bă shiàh dż.* |

Shocking!   *Mán shiàh rén dùh!*

Really amazing person.   *Shiàh shiàh jiòw.*

Freak.   *Chée juāng ì fú.* *

   * Person who wears outlandish clothes or has an
   outlandish hairdo.

Foreign ghost or devil (insult). *Yáng guǎy-dž.* *

   * Usually for Western Caucasians.

Foreigner.   *Wài-guó-rén.*
                                   Lǎu wài. *

   * Literally means "old foreigner." If someone Chinese
   calls you "old foreigner," you may respond by calling
   them "old Chinese," *lǎu Jōng.*

Yankee.   *Yáng-rén.*

Black person.   *Hāy-rén.* *

Red person.   *Hóng-rén.* *

White person.   *Bái-rén.* *

Yellow person.   *Hwáng jǒng rén.* *

   * The Chinese refer to themselves and other East

Asians as *Hwáng jŏng rén* (meaning yellow-type people) but usually refer to other races without the *jŏng* word. If one refers to them simply as *Hwáng rén,* one will be corrected. Therefore, I refer to my own race using the word *jŏng* as it seems to be more respectful.

It's a good thing that.	*Hŏw zài.**

* Literally means "it's lucky for you that..." For example, It's lucky for you that when you lost your wallet there wasn't any money in it.

Don't be like that!	*Biéh jùh yàng!*
Fierce, really awesome!	*Lì-hài!**

* This is a commonly used phrase and well worth remembering.

Say it again.	*Zài shuō í-bièn.*
A liars true intent.	*Jūn mièn-mòo.*
Don't waste your energy doing useless things!	*Shúng shŭng bà!*
It's bizarre if it's true!	*Tsái guài!*
Junior high school girl.	*Huáng máu yāh-tó.*
That hurts!	*Hŭn tòng!*

I'm not sure.	*Wǒ bú chùay dìng.*
He/she/it's gone!	*Tā zǒ lùh!*
There's so many people!	*Hǒw duō rén!*
Hidden.	*Duó chěe lái.*
Lively, exciting, good time.	*Rèr-nòw.*
Too early!	*Tài zǒw!*
Too late!	*Tài wǎn!*
Late.	*Chér-dòw lùh.*
No one is there.	*Dō máy yǒ rén.*
Too much!	*Tài duō lùh!*
Too little!	*Tài shǎu lùh!*
He/she/it came back.	*Tā yò lái lùh.*
Embarrassed to death.	*Shōu sž rén lùh.*
Old-fashioned.	*Lùo oǒ lùh.*
Exaggeration.	*Kuāh jāng.*

Too exaggerated!	*Tài Kuāh jiāng lùh.*
The difference is too exaggerated!	*Chà tài duō!*
You're kidding!	*Kāi wán-shiàu!*
Overexerted (done too much so that you are going crazy).	*Huēn lùh tó.*
Person who works extremely hard to do something (working, chasing women, exercising, etc.), so much so that he cares about nothing else.	*Pîn mìng.* *Gōng-dzùo kuáng.*

I'VE GOT THE MUNCHIES!

Are you hungry?	*Nǐ èr lùh mà?*
I'm starving!	*Wǒ èr sž lùh!*
I'm hungry.	*Wǒ èr lùh.* *Wǒ dù-dž èr lùh.**

* Literally means "my stomach is hungry."

No, I'm not.	*Wǒ bú èr.*
I'm not very hungry	*Wǒ bú tài èr.*
I want to eat.	*Wó shiǎng chēr.*
I don't want to eat.	*Wǒ bú yòw chēr.*
Are you thirsty?	*Ní kěh mà?*
I'm thirsty.	*Wǒ kó-kǔh.*
I'm not thirsty.	*Wǒ bù-kǔh.*

I'm not very thirsty.	*Wǒ bú tài kǔh.*
I don't want to drink.	*Wǒ bú yòw hūh.*
I want to drink.	*Wǒ yòw hūh.*
Have you ordered?	*Ní diěn tsài lùh mà?*
Waiter.	*Shàu yiéh.** *Shiǎu dì.*** *Shiēn shūng.****

* Formal.

** Informal, and is for young men.

*** Means sir.

Waitress.	*Shiǎu mày.** *Shiáu jiěh.***

* Informal, and means little sister.

** Formal, and means Miss.

Menu please.	*Tsài-dān máh-fán i-shìah.*
I'll order for us.	*Wǒ lái diěn tsài.*
Would you like a drink?	*Ní shiǎng hūh ǐng-liàu mà?*

Are you drunk?   *Nǐ dzuày-lùh mà?*

I'm drunk.   *Wǒ hūh dzùay lùh.*

Drink more!   *Duō hūh ì-diěn.***

     *** A polite way to refuse is to say *Suáy-ì.*

I drank too much.   *Wǒ hūh tài dūo lùh.*

Don't drink so much!   *Shǎu hūh diěn!*

I've got a hangover.   *Wó sù dzuày lùh.*

Smells delicious!   *Wén chǐ-lái hǔn
                        shiāng!*

It looks delicious!   *Kàn chǐ-lái hún hǒw
                        chēr!*

Let's start eating!   *Kāi-dòng lùh!*

Help yourself.   *Dʐ-jǐ lái.*

This is delicious.   *Jùh-gùh hún hǒw chēr.*

Try eating some.   *Chēr kàn kàn.*

I don't like it very much. *Wǒ bú tài shǐ-huān.*

What would you like to drink?	*Ní shiǎng hūh diěn shém-mùh?*
Beer.	*Pí-jiǒu.*
Wine, whiskey, etc.	*Jiǒu.*
Coffee.	*Kāh-fāy.*
Juice.	*Guǒ jēr.*
Soda.	*Chèe shuǎy.*
Water.	*Kāi shuǎy.**

* Means boiled water.

____ for me.	____ *shèr wǒ dùh.*
____ for him/her.	____ *shèr tā dùh.*

I want what he's having.   *Wó diěn gūn tā í-yàng
                            dùh tsài.*

It's expensive.   *Hǔn guày.*

It's cheap.   *Hǔn pién-i.*

Cheers!   *Gān bāy!**

    * Means "dry your cup."

This is awful.   *Jùh-gùh nán chēr sž
                            lùh.**

    *Sž means death and the nuance is that the food is
so bad it will kill you.

Eat more!   Duō *chēr diěn!*

Please give me a little   *Chǐng gáy wǒ duō ì-
  more.   diěn.*

Are you full?   *Nǐ chēr bǎu lùh mà?**

    * Sometimes said as a friendly greeting.

I'm full.   *Wó bǎu lùh.*

I'm not full.   *Wǒ hái máy bǎu.*

I ate too much.   *Wǒ chēr tài duō lùh.*

An Affair

Lover.   *Aì-rén.**

> * In mainland China this means wife or husband, but in other countries it means lover or mistress. Don't make the mistake of calling someone's wife their mistress.

Electrifying sensation of   *Chù dièn.**
love at first sight.

> * *Dièn* literally means electricity.

Electrifying talk of love.   *Lái dièn.*
(Usually after meeting
and falling in love.)

Old cows eat tender grass.   *Lǎo níou chēr nùn tsów.**

> * This refers to older men chasing younger women.

Man trying to catch a   *Diòw mǎ dž.*
woman.

Woman trying to catch a rich man.	*Diòw kǎi dż.*
Rich man.	*Yǒ chíen rén.*
Rich woman.	*Fù jiāh nǔu.*
Miss.	*Shiáu-jiěh.*
Sir.	*Shiēn-shūng.*
Single man.	*Dān-shēn hàn.*
Single woman.	*Dān-shēn nǔu láng.*
Single person.	*Dān-shēn gùay dźu.**

* Means rich, happy person.

Old single man (never married).	*Dǎ guāng-gùen.*
Playboy.	*Hwāh hwāh gōng dż.* *Hwāh shîn luó bùo.*
You are very cute.	*Nǐ hún kǔh aì.*
You are very pretty.	*Ní hǔn piòw-liàng.*
You are very beautiful.	*Nǐ hún mǎy.*

Very charming.	*Hŏw mí rén.*
You are so sexy!	*Ní hŏw shìng-găn!*
You have a beautiful body!	*Nĭ-dùh shūn-tsái hún măy!*
You have beautiful eyes!	*Nĭ-dùh yiĕn-gîng hún măy!*
Beautiful lady.	*Máy niŭ.*
Handsome guy.	*Swài gūh.*
You changed your hairstyle.	*Nĭ bièn făh-shíng lùh.*
I want to know more about you.	*Wó shiăng gèng liáu-jiéh nĭ.*

I like you!	*Wó shǐ-huān nǐ!*
Do you like ____ girls/boys?	*Ní shǐ-huān ____ niǔ-hái/nán-hái mà?*
Chinese.	*Jōng guó.*
American.	*Máy guó.*
I'm crazy about you!	*Wǒ wày nǐ fōng-kwáng!*
I'd like to take you out (on a date).	*Wǒ shiǎng chíng nǐ chū-lái.*
Would you like to dance?	*Ní shiǎng tiòw-wǔ mà?*
Would you accompany me?	*Páy wó hǒw mà?*
I'll accompany you home.	*Wǒ sòng nǐ hwáy jiāh.*
I miss you.	*Wó shiáng nǐ.*
I want you.	*Wǒ yòw nǐ.*
Close your eyes.	*Bì-shàng yiěn-gîng.*
Open your eyes.	*Jūng kāi yiěn-gîng.*

Kiss me!	*Wén wǒ!* * *Chîn wǒ!* **

* For lovers only.
** For anyone.

Bad breath.	*Kǒ-tsòu.*
Really stinks.	*Hǔn tsòu.* *Tsòu sž rén.* *

* Means "the stench will kill people."

Hug me!	*Bàu wǒ!*
I am yours.	*Wǒ shèr nǐ-dùh.*
You are mine.	*Nǐ shèr wǒ-dùh.*
I'm so happy!	*Wó hǒw kāi-shîn!*
Stay here.	*Lióu shiàh lái.*
Come close to me.	*Kòw jìn wǒ.*
What are you doing?	*Nǐ dzài dzùo shém-mùh?* *Nǐ dzài gàn shém-mùh?* *

* Rude or coarse if said harshly.

I want to make love.	*Wó shiǎng dzùo aì.*
Excellent (all right)!	*Hǒw jí lùh!*
No way!	*Bù shíng!*
I don't want to get pregnant.	*Wǒ bú-yòw huái-yuìn.*
Is today safe for you?	*Jîn-tiēn shèr nǐ-dùh ān-chúen chēe mà?*
Are you using protection?	*Ní yǒ bì-yùìn mà?*
Please use protection.	*Chíng nǐ dài báu-shiěn tàu.**

> * Means "please wear a condom."

Condom (rubber).	*Báu shǐen tàu.*
Do you have your period?	*Ní yǒ yuèh-shèr mà?*
Are you on the rag?	*Ní yǒ yuèh-jîn mà?*
I've got my period.	*Lì-jiàh lái lùh.* *Wó yǒ nùh-gùh.**

> * Means I've got "that."

Is this your first time?	*Nǐ shèr dì í-tsż mā?*

Male virgin.	*Zài shèr nán.*
Female virgin.	*Chú-niǔ.*
Old virgin.	*Lǎu chù-niǔ.* *

* Insulting term for old, unmarried woman.

Take your ____ off.	*Tuō-shìah nǐ-dùh ____.*
Clothes.	*Ī-fù.*
Coat.	*Dà-î.*
Shirt.	*Chèn-shān.*
Bra.	*Shiōng-jòw.*
Pants.	*Kù-tŝz.*
Dress.	*Yáng-juāng.*

Underwear.   *Này-kù.*

Shoes.   *Shiéh-tŝz.*

Body.   *Shūn-tí.*

Hair.   *Tó-făh.*

Eyes.   *Yiěn-jīng.*

Ears.   *Ěr-duō.*

Lips.   *Dzŭay-chúen.*

Breasts.   *Shiōng-bù.*
                            Dà năi mā.*
                            Poāh bàh. *

* Mean "big tits." *Dà năi mā* is for a woman whose specialty is giving milk.

   Năi-nài.**

** *Năi-nài* also means grandmother. Sometimes men ask women if it would be all right to kiss their *năi-nài*. *Năi* also means milk.

Nipple.   *Mî-mî tó.*
                            Rŭ-tó.
                            Năi-tó.

Rear end (ass).	*Twén-bù.* *Pì-gù.*
Navel.	*Dù-chée.*
Vagina.	*Īng-dòw.*
Penis.	*Īng-jīng.*
Testicles.	*Gōw-wán.*
Your ____ is/are so (big/small)!	*Nǐ-dùh ____ hǔn (dàh/shiǎu)!*
Touch me!	*Pòng wǒ!* *Muō wǒ.*
Don't touch me!	*Bú-yòw pòng wǒ!*
Don't touch me there!	*Bú-yòw pòng wǒ nà-lǐ!*
Don't do that!	*Bú yòw jùh yàng-dż!*
Stop!	*Tíng-jù!*
I'm a little nervous.	*Wó yǒ dién jǐn-jāng.*
Don't be nervous!	*Bú yòw jǐn-jāng.*
I'm afraid.	*Wó hǔn pàh.*

What are you afraid of?	*Pàh shém-mùh?*
Don't worry about it.	*Bú yòw dān shîn.*
Bite me!	*Yów wǒ!*
Lick me!	*Tién wǒ!*
Blow me!	*Shî wǒ!*
Softer.	*Shiǎu lì ì-diěn.* *Chîng ì-diěn.*
More tender.	*Wēn-ró ì-diěn.*
Stronger.	*Dàh-lì ì-diěn.*
Missionary style.	*Jèng-cháng tǐ-wày.*
Girl on top.	*Chǐ chúng tǐ-wày.*
Doggie style.	*Hò-bày shèr.* *Hò-bày tǐ-wày.*
Have you cum?	*Nǐ gōw-chów lùh mà?*
Not yet!	*Hái máy!*
I haven't cum!	*Wǒ hái máy gōw-chów!*

| Oh no! | *Aì-yò!* |
| I'm cumming! | *Wǒ kwài gōw-chów lùh!* |

Oh no!   *Aì-yò!*

Orgy.   *Záh-jiōw.*

I'm cumming!   *Wǒ kwài gōw-chów
                        lùh!*

I've cum.   *Wǒ gōw-chów lùh.*

I feel good!   *Wó hów shuǎng!**

   * Usually said after sex.

You do it so well!   *Nǐ dzuò-dùh hún hǒw!
                        Ní hǔn lì-hài!*

I love you!   *Wǒ aì nǐ!*

I don't want to leave you!	*Wǒ bù-shiǎng lí-kāi nǐ!*
I can't live without you!	*Wǒ bù néng máy yó nǐ!*
One more time.	*Zài í-tsz.*
I'm pregnant.	*Wǒ hwái-yuìn lùh.*
Abortion.	*Duò-tāi.*
Let's get married!	*Wǒ-mèn jiéh-hwēn bà!*
I want to marry you!	*Wó shiǎng jiàh gáy nǐ!** *Wó shiǎng chíu nǐ!***
* For women only. ** For men only.	
I have a ____.	*Wó yǒ ____.*
I don't have a ____.	*Wǒ máy yǒ ____.*
I want a ____.	*Wǒ yòw ____.*
I don't want a ____.	*Wǒ bú-yòw ____.*
Girlfriend.	*Niǔ-púng-yǒ.*
Boyfriend.	*Nán-púng-yǒ.*
Wife.	*Tài-tài.*

Husband.	*Shiēn-shūng.**

  * Also means Sir.

I don't love you!	*Wǒ bú ài nǐ!*
I can't go out with you anymore!	*Wǒ bù néng zài gūn nǐ chū chìu!*
I've got another lover.	*Wǒ ài-shàng lìng-wài í-gùh rén.*
I'm jealous of him/her.	*Wó hǔn jì-dù tā.*
Let's end our relationship!	*Jiěh-sù wǒ-mèn-dùh gūan-shî bà!*
I've got a sexual disease!	*Wǒ jòng biōw!*
I've got ____.	*Wó yǒ ____.* *Wǒ dúh-dòw lùh ____!**

  * This usage implies that someone gave it to the person.

You gave me ____!	*Nǐ chúan-rǎn ____ gáy wǒ lùh!* *Ní bǎ____chuán-rán gáy wǒ lùh.*

AIDS.   *Ài dʒ bìng.*

Herpes.   *Pòw-jŭn.*

Gonorrhea.   *Lín-bìng.*

Syphilis.   *Máy-dú.*

Whore, prostitute.   *Jì-niŭ.*

MAKING WAR

I hate you!	*Wó tău-yièn nǐ!*
I loathe you!	*Wǒ hùn nǐ!**

* Very strong statement and is seldom used.

I'll kill you!	*Wǒ yòw shāh-diòw nǐ!*
You've gone too far!	*Tài guò fèn!*
Shut up!	*Jù kǒ!* *Bì dzǔay!*
Don't speak!	*Biéh shuō lùh!*
Listen to me!	*Tîng wǒ shuō!*
Get the hell out of here!	*Gwěn chū chìu!**

* Means "roll away."

I'm a bit angry (pissed off)!	*Wó yǒ ì-dién hǔo dàh!*

What do you do for a living?	*Nǐ dzòah shém-mùh gōng-dzòah?*
I'm mad as hell!	*Wó hǔo dàh lùh!*
Calm down!	*Lěng-jìng ì-diěn!*
What the hell are you doing?	*Gàn shém-mùh?*
Have you finished speaking yet?	*Shuō wán lùh máy yǒ?*
It's none of your business!	*Máy yǒ nǐ-dùh shèr!*
Damn it!	*Gāi sž!*
Don't complain!	*Bú yòw bàu-yuèn!*
Stop screwing around!	*Biéh nòw lùh!*
You deserve it!	*Huó-gāi!*
Leave me alone!	*Bú yòw guán wǒ!*
Don't bother me!	*Biéh fán wǒ!*
Stop bothering me!	*Ráu lùh wǒ!*
Nagging person.	*Luō-sùo.*

Person who is always criticizing and nagging others.	*Láu dòw.*
Be polite!	*Kèh-chèe diěn!*
The noise is killing me!	*Tsáu sž rén lùh!*
Don't come to find me!	*Biéh jów wǒ!*
Forget it!	*Swàn lùh bà!*
Who do you think you are?	*Nǐ swàn láu-jǐ?*
You don't know your own shortcomings!	*Mǎ bù jēr lién cháng, hó-dž bù jēr pì-gù hóng!**

* Literally means "A horse doesn't know his face is long; a monkey doesn't know his ass is red."

Stuck up, arrogant person.	*Hów juǎi.*
You are a ____!	*Nǐ shèr gùh ____!*
No, you're a ____!	*Nǐ tsái shèr gùh ____!*
Good-for-nothing person.	*Nōw-jǒng.*
You are nothing.	*Nǐ bú shèr dōng-shi.*

Stupid.   *Bùn.**
                                   Bùn dàn.**

    * Adjective.
    ** Noun.

Person who pretends he   *Juāng swàn.*
   doesn't know anything.

Crazy.   *Fōng-dž.*

Sick.   *Yǒ bìng.*

Not normal.   *Bú jèng-cháng.*

Daydreaming.   *Dzùo bái-rèr-mòng.*

Dreaming.   *Fāh dāi.*

You're screwed up.   *Yǒ máu-bìng.**

    * This means something that is OK sometimes and at
    other times out of order. For example, a broken
    machine.

Weird.   *Chée-guài.*

This is too weird.   *Muò míng chée miòw.*

Weird guy   *Guài tāi.*

Horny guy.   *Sùh-láng.* *

    * literally means colored wolf.

Pervert (mentally sick person). *Bièn-tài.*

Pig.   *Jū-bā jièh.* *

    * Women's talk—for someone you can't stand.

Fat person.   *Chèe-yó-tŏng.*

Loves to eat.   *Aì chēr guăy.*

Skinny (like a monkey).   *Shòu-pí-hó.*

Fat-legged woman   *Luó-buò twǎy.*
  (has legs that look like
  carrots).

Moron.	*Bái-chēr.*
"Electrical shortage in the brain."	*Duǎn-lù.*
IQ of zero.	*Aî-kîu líng dàn.*
Bimbo.	*Èr bái wǔ.**

* Literally means the number two hundred fifty.

For a woman, the number 38.	*Sān-bā.*
For a man, the number 49.	*Sì-jiǒu.*
Stingy.	*Lìn-sùh.*
Big mouth.	*Dàh dzǔay-bā.*
Gossiper, blabber-mouth.	*Duō dzǔay.*
	Cháng-shúh-fù.*
	Cháng-shúh-nán.**

* For Woman.
** For Man.

Useless person.	*Fày-wù.*
Bad guy (will do anything for money).	*Hùen-hùen.*
	Hùen-hùr.
Monster.	*Guài oò.*

Bad teenager.	*Shiǎu-tài-bǎu.*
	Lùo-chèr.*

    *Female.

Narrow-minded.	*Shiǎu shîn-yiěn.*
Disgusting.	*Ér-shîn.*
Very mean.	*Hǒw shiōng.*
You are coldhearted.	*Máy liáng-shîn.*
	Búo chíng-láng.*

    * Women's insult towards a man.

Extremely ugly.	*Tsǒu bā-guài.*
You should look in the mirror.	*Yiěh bú jòw jìn-dż nà.*
Old man.	*Lǎu shiēn shūng.*
Old woman.	*Lǎu-tài-tài.*
Homosexual.	*Tóng shìng lièn.*
Coward.	*Dán shiáu-guǎy.*
Miser.	*Shiǎu-chèe-guǎy.*

Lazy person.	*Lǎn duò chǒng.*
Person who never expresses his feelings.	*Dž-bì jèn.*
Unappreciative person (person who can't tell when others treat him well).	*Bù jēr hów-dǎi.*
Rash, reckless person.	*Bù jēr sž húo.*
Your conscience bothers you (you know you did wrong).	*Shîn-lǐ yó guǎy.*
Inside you know the truth (you know what you should rightfully do).	*Shîn-lí yǒ shù.*
I never want to see you again.	*Wǒ zài yǐeh bú yòw kàn dòw nǐ.*
I'm leaving!	*Wǒ yòw zǒ lùh!*
Screw you!	*Chìu nǐ dùh!*
Fuck-you!	*Tā mā dà!*
Fuck your mother!	*Gàn nǐ niáng! Tsàu nǐ mā!*

Bitch!	*Biǒw-dż!*
Bastard!	*Wáng-bā-dàn!**

    * Literally means "turtle's egg."

I'm sorry.	*Dwày bù chǐ.* *Bàu chìen.*
Please forgive me!	*Chíng nǐ yuén-liàng wǒ!*
I forgive you.	*Wǒ yuén-liàng nǐ.*
I can't forgive you!	*Wǒ bù núng yuén-liàng nǐ!*
I'll never forgive you!	*Wǒ yóng-yuěn bù yúen-liàng nǐ!*
I want to apologize.	*Wó shiǎng dòw-chìen.*
You'd better apologize.	*Nǐ dzùay hǒw dòw-chìen.*
Ok, but don't let it ever happen again.	*Hǒw, dàn-shèr bú-yòw zài fāh-shēng jùh jǒng shèr-chíng.*
Don't do it again!	*Shiàh bù wáy lì!*

Ok, you're right.	*Swàn nǐ dwày.*
OK, you win.	*Swàn nǐ íng.*
OK, I lose.	*Swàn wǒ sū.*
You are/were____.	*Nǐ shèr ____.*
I am/was____.	*Wǒ shèr ____.*
He/she/it was____.	*Tā shèr ____.*
Right.	*Dwày dùh.*
Wrong.	*Tsuò lùh.*
Karma.	*Bàu-ìng.*

What goes around comes around:

For evil things.	*Èr yǒ èr bàu.*
For good things.	*Shàn yǒ shàn bàu.*

VOGUE
EXPRESSIONS

I'm ugly but I'm tender.

Wó hún tsŏu, kŭh-shèr wó hŭn wēn-ró.*

   * Usually said by men.

Chase women (look for a girlfriend).

Bá mă dż.

Begin to work hard to accomplish something.

Fāh biōw.*

   * This is often said of men chasing women.

Sexy lady.

Jèn-diĕn.

Very cute (fashionable).

Hŭn kìu.

Person completely out of style (geek, hick).

Hŭn pòw.

Stupid-looking person.

Hŭn lú.

A genius may look stupid.   *Dàh jèr rùo yú.**

> * This is an old expression (not exactly in vogue), but is a nice comeback if anyone ever accuses you of being stupid-looking.

You've solved a problem.   *Bǎi píng.*

I want to make love.   *Wó shiáng dǎ pòw.*

Wrinkles by eyes.   *Yú-wǎy-wén**

> * In the West such wrinkles are known by the slang "crow's feet" as if stepped on by such a bird, but the Chinese don't see it that way. They envision a fish whose body is your eye and whose tail is the wrinkles. The expression literally means "fish-tail wrinkles."

For the love of baseball!

Many Chinese love to play baseball—so much so that they've come to think of many things in baseball-related terminology—just like Americans.

First base.   *Ì-láy-dǎh.*
  (Got a date.)

Second base.   *Èr-láy-dǎh.*
  (Held hands.)

Third base.
(Kissed and fooled
around a bit.)

Sān-láy-dǎh.

Home run.
(Made love.)

Chúen-láy-dǎh.
Bún-lay-dǎh.

Three strikes.
(Date was refused.)

Sān jèn.
Sān-jî-wày-jòng.

Pop fly.
(Your near home run
was caught and thus
a possibly successful
love affair was abruptly
terminated)

Jiēh shiāh.

A Rating System

The Chinese are extremely polite people and are such even when young men are rating women. The following is used by men to categorize women by appearance.

She is very beautiful. (Said of extremely beautiful women.)	*Tā hǔn piòw-liàng.*
She is very cute. (Said of women of moderate beauty.)	*Tā hún kǔh-aì.*
She is very patriotic. (Said of plain-looking women.)	*Tā hǔn aì-guó.*
She obeys the rules well. (Said of ugly women.)	*Tā hún shǒ guāy-jǐu.*
Her writing is very beautiful. (Said of extremely ugly women.)	*Tā shiěh dż hǔn piòw-liàng.*